*Trees Before
Abstinent
Ground*

Also by Peter Larkin

Enclosures
Prose Woods
Pastoral Advert
Terrain Seed Scarcity
Slights Agreeing Trees
Sprout Near Severing Close
Rings Resting The Circuit
What the Surfaces Enclave of Wang Wei
Leaves of Field *
Lessways Least Scarce Among *
Imparkments (The Surrogate Has Settled)
Give Forest Its Next Portent *
City Trappings (Housing Heath or Wood)
Introgression Latewood *

Wordsworth and Coleridge: Promising Losses

* *Titles from Shearsman Books*

Peter Larkin

Trees Before Abstinent Ground

Shearsman Books

First published in the United Kingdom in 2019 by
Shearsman Books
50 Westons Hill Drive
Emersons Green
BRISTOL
BS16 7DF

Shearsman Books Ltd Registered Office
30–31 St. James Place, Mangotsfield, Bristol BS16 9JB
(this address not for correspondence)

www.shearsman.com

ISBN 978-1-84861-675-2

Copyright © Peter Larkin, 2019.

The right of Peter Larkin to be identified as the author
of this work has been asserted by him in accordance with the
Copyrights, Designs and Patents Act of 1988.
All rights reserved.

ACKNOWLEDGEMENTS

I thank the following magazines and their editors where extracts from some of these poems first appeared: *Amethyst, Blackbox Manifold, Free Verse, SNOW, Stride, Tears in the Fence.*

Enormous gratitude to Tony Frazer and Shearsman Books for once more publishing a collection of my recent work.

I am truly obliged also to Simon Lewty, Colin Lee Marshall, Emma Mason and G. C. Waldrep for reading and commenting on early drafts.

Contents

Possible
Wild Sticks

7

Enjoinment
Enter Tree

25

Trees
Feral for Light

47

Until
Under a Wood

69

Expressing
Trees by Default

91

POSSIBLE WILD STICKS

(Origin Log)

Thus, the tree branch was a possible stick before I think about it, will remain a stick when I no longer think about it, *ie*, there is an order of the in-itself in which the tree branch is by means of itself an elongated solid whose proper use is to obtain a goal. The reorganisation offers itself as the discovery of a pre-existing, true, objective property, which will never wear out.
Maurice Merleau-Ponty

How deceptive the size of a large pine! As you approach it, it looks only like a reasonable stick fit for the sill or the beams of an old-fashioned house. You apply your measures. The foot rule seems suddenly shrunk. Your umbrella is but half as long as it was.
Henry David Thoreau

It might have been a tree or pole; I think it is merely a way.
Gary Snyder

I

Begin what has arisen
in trees
by picking up
sticks

some trees are not known for their own good
but from their broods of stick

                                          sticks snap until they float off
                                   tree current: keep damping sticks
                                       towards a stream of tree
                                       but these webs are weirs

stick stillage pre-dates a branch's current wave,
both open verticals with no debt to height

                                   thin brittle instructibles of forest:
                           where you see dormancy in the stick
                               it hurdles outruns of horizon,
                                     legging it awake
                                  across symbolic peg

a stick's invention anticipates
(antequates) the already generated

                               blown branches sweep the stickground,
                                   pitting trees against their
                                     own prime derivatives

adept nature on all excrescences,
the reifications give off
vertically able conductors

                                          no oak ever grew
                            except to be concrete in stick,
              concerted in the distended quick of it

sturdy uplift of a branch broken straight,
a stick out of tree has its own stab
at branch   arborial stacks
stain an instrumental body
only at its verticality

                            rings in swirl where a branch was,
                                  lever its way through
                      harsh currents of vertical hunger
                              where there is to be this
                    premonition of clemency in stick

underwood does stay for
cracklings of forest   whichever
snap into lift was the more vertical,
extraction is from sticks of it stood

                            what rests on uprights can dismember
                                          but not disarm

lattice that lessens toward vertical task,
sticks of provision solely their
uprights' any spiritual increment
grateful
along stems gone rigid

                                        the distortion will diagonally thrive,
                                                      tooled to the ask

already condenses a prior disjoining
not a borrowing of tree canals
but the tenor of their hardened ducts

                                  the object tree gives mere sheaf
                                  to tautnesses, all its localisation
                                untethered but marking out in sticks,
                              to be non-shelf with all the strength
                                  of a tree's long single caution

tapestry of arrested twigs
at each stitch into stick   both
leap to growth but one
is steeped in the death
of its pliable lift

                                              no fresh dendritic nervure
                                            along its otherwise entire
                                                        anticipation

a forest shape sheds stick
direct on burdens of horizon,
lets swat at formatives to be offered:
thinning into stick by the same token
as pinning onto rise

                                every tree works out of huge mansions
                                stored in its growth but apparent stick
                                sets the first green joist

sticks for a skirt of heartwood,
their own brittle whirl is
direct unavoidance of pre-perished core,
the lure of every tree's before

                                if among smuts and starts
                                there has been no felling,
                                through outpaced long exception
                                all the slightings
                                of its non-extinction

an erect leap at horizon,
snip off crest and have
tree stalking whatever is
behind with whatever
is beyond it

                                praised off ground but vouching
                                for land, lately in the stick of it

II

Dried wood
the tool
kindled by stick

transformer active wicket,
skinny brackets foretell
the full girth of tree stump

posit sticks at soft adhesive surface
mediated by slow fruition friction,
soft spells pre-circuit hard branches:
if this is structure extract, it is a saliency map
on surface normals

that sticks were covered in leaves,
that branches will be levered away
(intact bruteness of sharepoint):
we no longer know which
of the two frequents a
fuller arbour, either request
is out of sequence

whose boughs accelerate until
prolonged by the interval stealth
of stick-reach: conventional
isolations of stick wealth

what ascends the tree-site
is a sense of branch: what ascended
branch was a sense of trunk: what incenses
trunk will be vertical
concussion (in rays of stick)

                                                    premature, disentire stiffness
                                                        strikes a flash off horizon,
                                        sands a telos way down its staff,
                                              smoothing (it smote) its yield
                                                    of vertical gravitation

separable ballast (picked
from uprights apart) speared
through an absolute beginning

                                                     prescript tree flux: it worked
                                        every one of its instants to stick,
                 showered forest onto the tenses of its materials

resumes snappy furtherances of future
sticks on the point of its edge sediment

                                        without these delayings of tree
                                          barrier (full tree barrage) no
                                        sticks could be a prime carrier

tree verticals on the divergence,
as uprights any plural is sole tree reference:
any upright assumption of tree isn't the normal
state of stick which space out
their deadwood arisen
horizontal livings

                                          vertical peak amid full horizontal gear,
                                          did share out what blunts to summit
                                                but had always recrowned a
                                                  graded acuteness in sticks

given that woods belt against
land-slack   to sound
a reach through an
overblown stick

                                        what is cut short by stick? the bare
                             stroke of a tree, or fully ripened grace
                                       of these non-renewables?

as stick by storm comes to walk
the ravaged spot   tree is a sword
to tree, a hilt for the stick-blade: once drawn,
any splitting cries for its mark

                                            sticks offer variable speed
                                  expenditures   darts of tree-flesh
                                    imprint (award) at bespoke horizon

no straightening is possible
beyond primaries of stick, they do
press what had attributed
capture to a negotiating
origin

                                          givens up to the very origin
                          of unpredictable confirmation, authentic
                                  stems of arousal fit their
                        transmissible burdens of instrument

if sticks were a harness they are
free of root-drag but baulk their own
height to weight: a meandering source
celebrates its co-solids   sticks frozen
into source, outlying the indicator

                                flat of the way there are no sticks
                                    to it, a tree living on verticals
                              lunges at once, may a shift in sticks
                              embody its height of commission:
                            fields its smoothest suture to have
                                  fallen into providing again

how tree is a woody implant jump-parted
by its own arrows of attire   surrogated
elsewhere, so set off in sticks,
the transitions of oak stalking ash

impossible to strip trees
once dense in stick, despite all
the instrumental legacies: the longer
a stick takes for polarity
(relays the dividers), the less
it was ever treeless

III

                Original trajectory
              moves a consecutive
                    in sticks, re-
                verticals present
                 how it proves

always choose the smaller
possible stick to forsake
(intend) a midmost

                                the stick possible not as tooling it
                                oftener than whole trees themselves
                                but their stability readily transportable

not yet posts from a credal trunk
nor its unfolding leaf beliefs
but darts of straight transfer

                                        parallel sticks upright
                          off a wounded bough on the diagonal,
                              affirms (abbreviates, indurates)
                          its vertical cordon in a curtain afloat

across sticks the truss of an advent:
it might be made into select prior cut,
the grace token offers its before-seed
to plead-rods of a time

                                    virtual staffing come to after-uses,
                          invites a tree's history into minor masks,
                                          its deepest rootal graft

the stick is linear incompletion
with slender co-remunerants, an
after-combination in time
with its pre-fuse within the core of tree

                                      only half-removal of what slipped
                                where it grew, except in the complete
                          givenness of stick to its travelling ledge

flat on the ground in full
symbolic plight, separate sticks
joint-hungry in structural reserve

                          such importability of tree is put in reserve,
                                not to be brought to but will walk again

not a free scene but over and above
sticks spending vertical re/lay,
lean exact trees walking into genesis

                                there is no stick-shift (pull-apart)
                              other than unstrafable tree which
                                  accords stick no spoiler tag

symbolics of tapering stick, such
a meta-instrument flickers tree,
the haven offer is core immensity
of micro-drift, macro-lift

                                        stick-heavy finals trembling
                                 off verticals, cleaving ahead of
                                            any beyond-branching

fetching a stick off a wrist of tree
whittled to what it imparts:
this one shift-ache is
what it offers to origin

                                            sticks not as a tree sector
                         (however primordially pre-cut) but
                               liables hanging off a core:
                               plentitude for the use of
                                 poor regularities, a
                                   leaned-on aspiracy
                                       of origin

blunting of finalities what goes
with what mounts a vertical on   acute
replay finals so resemble how
sticks snapped over (enjoined)
their without definition

                                        skeleton to periphery but
                                         not before its own
                                             vertical trial

what are tree uprights going
to mean (as gift) without
travelling their sense
of sticks?   until
symbol admission re-
cycles a sediment's
latest intention

                              stick material once in companion
                                    role asks for no further
                        rematerialisation of its straightness:
                                emergence is only taller
                                to take on burdens, proffer
                            a directionality of the pre-use

passive separation offers its frontal
elation, sticks of a poverty for use,
a prop to incessant horizon: leans
on the leave-ins of prayer

                                finger these sticks strong origins
                            no longer repletely (too far longer)
                      within the envelope of arboreal terracing

the pressure-cone off sticks runs
on a natural risk of origin,
tooled proto-shifters of gift

                    not adjacent enough for full
                    prop but will muster a cross-brace
                    interval at real tree fenestration,
                    mullions at a time:
                    no need now for *recumbent* expulsion

woodland comes from secondary
wood (vascular cambium) but as
going stickward to primaries,
its wands of origin

                    what is it lingers past the scant
                    of its non-absence?   only sticks
                    in a world can bear the weight of
                    tree-geometry, stand rations of origin
                    to let such unmade relations stiffen forward,
                    into the spares of invitation

a numinous scratches, sticks
of origin across the tree continuum:
how sticks breast a ground
is from no stain of wood
but a complexion of root

                    as guided leaf is no longer
                    forced to fletch on sticks, let them
                    be thrown towards
                    the formatives of primitive tree

unestranging ripe for
induration of further incitements
to symbol (however
crustless its applied verticals)

                                        larches filing slower
                                        (a little dimmer) their
                                  chosen recordings of sticks

that sticks *do* impinge
on what was too innocently
flush (horizonless)
with finitude

                                until I can hatch this foliage
                   prove a stick   from wondering roots
                                   to straight steps unstunned

what bites on stick
was originally what browses
on nothing quit

ENJOINMENT
ENTER
TREE

1

No injunction save enjoinment

How a joint counter-gains its tree

> diagonals ship out
> what a trunk allays
> intricated, broader
> than its dispersal
>
> heavy with tree-
> shoes for the
> call of joint

Where intruded grain cycles a knot

Fewer at its disposal

2

There is every niche in the jointure

The tree is integral stack at a joining behaviour

> performing any unbrace *in* the
> range of prayer, clears
> the status
>
> spirit firms up to
> pure finitude, until
> a time enjoins for
> horizoning the present

Roadside trees already a knee's amending avenue

A crook to a curve is a radius jacked beyond safe intent

3

What will jam a tree is unlike an enjoinment

> lightest crust at the lateral
> mark, tail of root

Crisp at joint, the salient ledge unlevering

Inelastic vectors of tree due true reach-out

> responsorium under
> no new quittance

A ligature within the specimen dealing apart

4

Stacked free-codings spool filaments off radius

> a tree is enjoined
> only as it waves forward
> at branches athwart

The trunk an ongoing valve for all its dearth

> at the enjoined meeting
> a bulking (baulking) from
> no further stalking

Pre-branch is post-rootal, untangles sockets of consent

5

Displacement instils a gauge, this is jointure unsuccumbing

Maximum key no longer at the root

>branches in joints (discaged)
>off trunks. We (they) do not
>rear. We were to be there
>afar or ago.

>only a fully clouded
>sky is junction-
>proof, joints
>still won't crowd
>a tree-bole

Nearer the non-spear of erect tree, branching bespeaks it

No linkless tree shall be left to collide with its own ceiling

6

A self-balancing tree of few intercepts

Thin terms (forest) newly encumbered a succulence of prayer

>thicken to the trunk
>of it, but persist to a
>steepness out of
>joint

A vascular purge freed up the grain of joint

Turns the insulation towards some sustaining filtered pedal

7

Lamed in the clearing, a joint is crotch not crutch

    tethers an old spine
    away from centre, the
    lateral dance (dome)
    crossing through
    its wrist arising

    in marks around
    branches hushed
    into joint, no shoot
    out of gear

At the push-off of reset sections

A deck for leafing the entrant currents

8

Jointing a single hub is not yet an axle-tree

A map from woods to trees the tissue at every joint

    at the unsnubbed jut
    some labyrinth of branch
    to recline the exception

    any arising is post-
    order traversing,
    heavy-headed
    but shaping
    no dead code

Inclines to the offer, the rub of jointure

Sealing a trunk the way a joint comes in, its stowage horizon

9

Entire green field of tree

Pinioned to injected spread, no one branch ahead

> joint is the pure
> taint of horizon,
> translates all other poor
> gifts of apportioning
>
> splay of rest and sway,
> no longer to be an
> anti-type requites
> this novelty

A joint in spine is a point diagonal in time

Arborist fretwork strings each duct across the entry

10

How does a joint arouse a defeated (reseated) landscape?

Stark bale-out of foliage

> in the cast of space
> its unvast base (joint
> by joint's imperative
> horizon): compare
> the lack of impounding
>
> heap-ordered
> at the choir of
> each node

One leaf to a tree is still a first for junction

Each least unbare solo shoot

11

Tree-dependent tender variables

Jointly lateral or vertical, let no pair be branchless

> detect *into* tree
> passive resolute joint:
> a tree is active base
> in full lens of a
> decent divergence
>
> each bolt towards tree-
> stubble instils me
> deeper into the gravel

Prefix a joint at every jolt

Never suspect from slim rejoinders the outward tree

12

A prayer opening at sight spends until sacral obstruction

A step away from berating its stale tree

> confess protuberances (a
> sea change) are tight enough
>
> address joints *along* tree,
> they are slender compressions
> of a steep departure,
> a ligature arriving
> too early for any
> specimen of coming apart

The serial instruction 'made to tree' finds the gap

Swirls a cone of prayer at enjoinment's nub

13

A neck might feel like a joint but can't broadcast its compressions

A tree's instep only rises at root, a use along every arching shoot

> true joint for bracing
> a lateral, no fork but
> sealed asymmetry at its
> branch-to-stem
>
> joints flex relative
> to the tree-house's own
> repudiation of tower

That the forest auditorium should not be aisleless

A joint nearest to root turning a corner

14

Wood mechanics helically unwind

Not free of the fear how it is joints unzip

> any assessment of
> join becomes a flange
> as internal crater
> not shown along
> the bone of countershaft
>
> fractal-like enhancing
> structures but each link
> moves to its single
> macro-swerve

No plethora of joint could outstare root myriads

What hubbub for a hormone to travel its internal distance

15

Too raw to confect joints into tree, they are a tree's *onto*

Interior for the seal they must breach, entire branch reparation

> stabilizers, even fixators
> but in deference
> to how a joint
> intersects a trunk
>
> with no other
> spine reversal
> than this surveying
> decorum of branch,
> stanches the outsweep

So as to re-enrol the swoop

Almost a rotation of entire corona

16

Unmoored   no appetite towards its aside

A diagonal swerve needs its issue above ground

> advice in my mind
> is a tree made of
> every joint I've
> reverted upon
>
> as a sensor of
> burdened givings
> this is how it skims
> the drop-weight
> of the lateral

Leave abyss a turn in the not-nothing, skimp no heartwood gate

An unappending residue (trunk) to swell the enjoinment

17

Which tree is enjoined to pitch a counter-tree?

Horizon will greet it to the apposition

> shelter is the employ-
> ment of a vertical
> to guide, trail
> its upright pre-
> ference across
> these outrights
>
> at its defence to
> defer only a symbol's
> patience, of its
> hollow-root entrance

How many side features under the pine-tree law?

Depart trunk and make for limb

The scramble (easement) a way to cheat-with, meet-with

18

'What gives' chafes until symbolic corona

No imbricant unless grained in the joint of it

> a generous default
> abyss glides pre-
> hardened, then
> releases at joint
>
> give it out in
> rootal sieve,
> syringe and plug

A core the less for what is spent along a shoot

That lessening freshly leases joint

19

Hard massing in tree loosens any joint before its bud

Expansively allows a curb to track its side-skin

> to orient the tree
> let it spiral its
> diagonal crumbs of
> earth, new hori-
> zontals give attachment
>
> a new horizon fore-
> angled the beseechment
>
> around a post-
> tangle (spray)
> of shoot

Arboreal versus terrestrial

The cursus (tree dial) is immemorial

20

Bulges until tenant enough for joint

Composite join to mimic the ructions of tree

> joint-tree is point
> parsimony for shaft
> seal seepage, gen-
> erous at the prong
>
> prompted weak wood
> onto tree, its laterals
> are temperate

Like a cylinder tapped into leaf, spun to the root

Girdle tree away from its starker habit

21

Layer of impartment amidships side-on projectile

Butting in and out of the protection

> embossed sector of
> real-world living
> trunk, the sanctuary
> a new recruit of
> givens upon given
>
> gathers across
> its antennae
> as driven
>
> if you wielded the
> legs of it, this
> is root finding its
> shoulder, so leaf
> derives arms

Diagonalising chamber (non-climber) recoups leakage of the process

Let it soak so a sheer crux of shelter

22

Careless of overhang but can determine (diagram) the probe-abilities

Best branch strength at first junction spent

> self-weight exerts
> compressive force, ex-
> pressive resource
>
> reinforces the region
> of its fleeter brace,
> more tenuous space

To a trunk admit tension, from a joint deep lateral invention

Base of frame towards wedged tenon, pits its contortion against split

23

Modulus of branch will string its open set, leaf at drag force

Reduces to slender ratio (recess) its beside-buckling

> watersprouting off old
> buried buds, weak but
> uncannily vertical
>
> stiffness juts it
> about, the transitional
> biomimetic its
> origin inspires,
> extracellular prayer

Adding how it stood in for idle wood

Report tree to branch per portion of root-swell

24

For a strain condition, resort to a speculative speckle pattern

The joint only secure amid unbreachable rasp

> no least harmonics
> under heavy windload,
> joint prominence
> will reimagine
> apical dominance
>
> lowest bracket
> stint, charge a
> joint for the state
> of the incline

No pads to rest against other than target tree

Know the remission at its prior corrugated trust

25

Any latent tenancy zone must be jointly kinematic

Mid-joint allowance of trends in trunk

> primitive colliders
> not needy enough
> to slice a knot

> main tree object
> abjures any rigid
> body component

Let its unlevelling rest, re-enjoin

Anchor the joists in a sport of retorting to horizon

26

At a compound to count down its numerate leaves

Given at joint no trees so attend their cloak

> an out-where of
> woods feathered at
> joint, a fledgling
> withinness with
> which they flaunt

> *articulatio*, shoulder
> to border, legging
> dovetail horizon,
> radical enjoinment
> at a knuckle's re-
> lief, its long
> thigh schedule

A whole ladder of bark bids for a joint's emplacement

Translation value is fellow bracement along a curve

27

First one tree than another's horizon across singular degrees

At a junction no two things except shared diagonal pressure

> tree at an address
> of other stays, jutt-
> ing not jussive

> pulse thrown to a
> garbled given, sown
> and semi-riven, para-
> digm unpercussive

Filters the convergence of a further, former verve

Leaves recoil, it is lignin stirring the brief weave

28

Rumble the wandering, a branch divagates at each echo of joint

A crib-like prayer had rocked one rib

> ontology of tree-
> speck, alliances of
> crust and breast,
> joinal apprentice

> the joints won't be
> snubbed as a branch
> can, the incentive has
> twig trounce twig

Latent stumble, over a crutch to find the attenuation

Transgrounding, offer an arm less its thrust

29

Any joint will scar where lanced by branch

Given, ungathered, aboard this collateral bending

> a prayer of depart-
> ure tells of tree
> startled back to
> joint, its symptom
> (nodule) of spirit
> up to its arms
>
> once you touch
> the real, project an
> inner resistance
> jointed on its scale
> (ladder) of assault

Infinite provisionality accords finite restitution, actual sacral

No rival jog at mainstem, already the prayer of anticipation

30

A joint doesn't *fork* from apex, keeps its conversion to come

A vertical aside boldly broader than *climbing* to dependence

> extenuate began
> gives lateral socket
> the appointment,
> shapes every tree
> across it, ad-
> joins and sets out
>
> enter arborial re-
> entrenchment, what
> a trunk won't open to
> from its steeper insides

No clean take-out unless the horizon-bundle fully seen

Enjoinment credits its tree further than by root

31

Scarcely a joint on the run from first negotiations

Enters an abyss of trunk, spiry ventricles shrink the root-load

    joint sensory burden
    at given edge,
    secondary crest
    pro-possibles
    from undersourced
    intimate diagonals

    wild proliferation
    savingly rewards
    its sparse tent,
    rejoices the entity

    co-intrusive
    pact of thriving
    a locked hinge

Last incursion, integral (hazard of joint) contemporary

Between earth and world only mutual shelter enjoins the ratio

32

Whatever opens a joint by no swing of a gate

Subjoint re-entrants, unrepentant, dia-ascendant

> the gist of a join
> is how it might
> never imagine
> a strained bough
>
> its contingent of branch-
> ing circumstance, the
> joint of it bearing,
> not rearing, gifts

Worn in extenso outside its alignment

How a tree is incarnate, that its trunk might have thumbs

Envoi

Deodar: bark-to-rib becomings rise until joint

Beech: glacial advantage, joints its smooth lanes

Douglas fir: micro-joints (close-grown) take major pecks out of trunk

Scots pine: what falls, umbrellaed, over its joints

Scots pine: joints self-appalled, blink at their portions

Holm oak: crocodile tiles, snaps along outgoing joint

Ash: shingle across swathe, bathes in joint

Juvenile ash: chalky fleck, until stripes *are* jointed

Oak: its whole guise enabling joint surprise

Sessile oak: slippery beside joint, virtual fork, but joinery unperturbed

Cherry: horizontal rings spooling along diagonal adjoinment

Apple: knobs of forgotten joint await the fresher fruit

TREES FERAL
FOR LIGHT

In the northern hemisphere, branches growing on the southern side of a tree will express themselves horizontally, lending the body of the tree an asymmetrical profile, with dense vertical branches to the north, and grasping, open-armed boughs to the south.

While humans and most complex animals orient to the horizon, trees have organised their lives vertically. The 'front' of a tree … is its efflorescing canopy, questing sunward. The tree's growth is happening along a dimension, the vertical; and yet is unfolding and ramifying into branches contrapuntally, polyvocally…

                Matthew Battles, *Tree*, 75, 103-4.

among the heavens where light's myth forms its stretches denting the eye along the ethics of matter   vertical along a crest of instability: translucent canopies shade tension

                Mark Dickinson

mais rester fidèle a si peu que la lumière

                Pierre Voélin

1

Light's gift stretches its relays along graphics
of frame and divide, forks a different
bringing

                Not straining for light but stirring it into their
                formals   matters of light at last
                ethereal amid tree-fetch

        a tree's outline,
        its outliers of spine
        do not feign light

        weave closer, adventing
        folds of light, won't
        sheerly ingest

        finds meekness in
        imperfect affliction,
        luminescent curves
        as if swivelling
        off a rind

                A crown's history by the different facets
                of extraordinary orientation

The wood clots deeper in its schematics, asymmetric
or misshapen in concord to site

2

Consider a tree plasticity stark within the
hereditary current   a larger wave-count easing out
concise symmetries of blocked tree

> To countenance the drag of recognition,
> memory's disfeature mantled in
> sunlight

> no uninterrupted sample
> shape from sapling to
> veteran   contests branch
> knotted onto the light
> of its corrugations

> a sky in vertical
> widens an horizon
> wrinkle the sun

> nothing less
> energises from
> sight   a guided
> tree-form
> refracts back

>> So that light might reface lineaments of the
>> branches' broken customs, as once they speared
>> through the lateral fires of sunset

Approach tree to seek (sink) a light entailing its
token, caught between lift and breadth.
The unreclusive touch from an ending's
extract   trees frozen onto adaptive
summer

3

Emission of shape gazes a session of the vertical,
averting horizon until the issue is
fully photo-corrective

                    Where horizontals only partly grieve, given to
                    whole counter-swathes of light, ascriptive
                    diagonals were no decoy

        single tree expressive
        long lamp off
        forest flash

        how a tree recruits
        light keeping its
        graded retortion
        aglow

        a site of skewed
        transfer placed
        on balance
        at lit tree

        light for green,
        feral at the tree-
        monumental
        led to portions of
        light, ferreted out
        from the smarts
        of reception

                A symbolic entanglement highly shared most
                pared from pivotal trigger   lit asides
                don't need to tarnish their sky-arm
                slender vertical

Trees won't harry the light heavenward but re-
dedicate an unshed midst of concrete verticals, the
prayer-accelerant at a compact rift
luminant

4

Habits of light what a tree wears on its steepness,
rim-paradable glades of inclination, infinitely
slow oscillation

> A flicker of limbs lit across a land's long
> graze, scraped pasture invites a nondescript tree
> wilding its own before the barest light

> to launch into light
> to scold a leaf
> with all the links,
> not stop short
> but gaze
> (gate it) tall

> what are the
> spares of light?
> radiant gauges'
> upper gameplay?

> where are the attestive
> paucities?   A tree
> is full light unsated,
> heavily fated
> entire forest task

> > How can these horny beacons, given to
> > stabbing, affix, inflict themselves
> > with light?

Light-demanders are not sun-commoners,
spell out their summits along
minor probes of gift

5

The culture (tree variable verticals) of light
is central querk   no less an array of transitions,
estrangements, intimacies

>A tree's splenetic propensity to rapture
as much light as possible   a gene's sheer
completion in light/shade ratios still a
rocked frame

>elective light sits
for the nearest
tree   mosaic
of spectral environs,
not laying rays
between but *at*
the bunches of
detection

>photon transport
across hybrid
inception trends
towards a highly
ridged attraction

>any cradled
summit must
spring from
a quit foremost

>>Self-casting onto relations of light even before
it has a costing of shadow and root   feral
negotiation through shields and welters

What dances in brief light a slewed life?   trees no longer
random once thumbed through for alcoves of
concentric dazzle

6

Light spoils no two trees alike,
they assemble each other's near-extinction
radiance   then see how the spires are
extreme formal residue
strictly residing

                Post-determined by an invariance of light
                in movement   only vicinity subsides into
                retaining the divagations   sculpting indirect
                (vertical) desire

        assume a tree
        once a
        day learning
        its profile

        close enough
        to light to
        truncate its
        secret, all forest
        initially soft
        on target

        falling onto a
        cadence which
        creases with the
        tempo of light

                Light gives no reprieve from feral engineering,
                a calculus of macular response, patchwork
                of architecture in feed

The same sun is good for branch-mien and extended
leaf release

7

Upper growth doesn't follow lighting a probe, a negative
geotrope pulls dire sky, fans another radical field-glow
along the vertical lane

                A tree sender delivers high, then locks onto
                fallow light, slender constancies
                of atmosphere

        what offers its
        own salience,
        bewilderment of
        outcrop once
        dressed, lifted
        from intense
        coruscation

        old-fault trees
        steeped in feral
        contention, they
        repack a dappled
        plight of myriad
        material

        solar residue
        micro-settled
        sifts an energy
        decorum, the
        geospatial taunt

                If I could detect the veering of a bough off
                a brow of light   twig behaviour nothing
                of a filter, but brushes towards such
                a post-clamouring

If stalling northwards an upward heaven, southerly
horizontals pitch a gantry off diagonal
alighting

8

Light/shade pleads for the trees' assent strutting
their frame joys, a ferally deep
orientation

                      As though sunrise lent boxes around grills
                      of counter-shadow, further fleetings
                      of light

            what towers into
            heaven is lowered
            onto light

            feral scrappiness
            at a mild dose
            framed towards
            striplings of
            focus

            dark green lenses,
            every tree held
            to a telescoping
            of its account

            where light re-
            bores the
            orientation,
            the twist is
            an entire frame's
            reboning

>Sun and wind teach forest its preliminary lobby,
>guide its portals to respire deeper
>corridors of outcome

Light does eventually chide the widest asymmetries,
lets a tree flock to its ramification

9

A leap into the sky primed by the sun's first
assault   prints out in seasonal writhe, eventual
fame of trees

                      As a forest bunches its two-dimensional,
                      unidirectional multiple, it shifts from
                      riddle to fable

          a single spangle
          rotates the
          spokes of beech

          no hindlight
          other than the
          upface of a
          remote clarity

          sifting evergreen
          harms (pine
          clamour) from
          successives
          of light

                      Oak backs stark at the rear of light tossing up
                      for a poverty of the vertical

A stairwell ray is fairest tier in such compressed
copses   light wrecks the symmetry of trees
from its perfect deck of lift

10

Asymmetry as light-centering, the new ask of a
forsaken prayer that took

>   Allow forest its heliocritical spokes,
>   flickering compensation where it never
>   adjourned the light

>   to exemplify, not
>   amplify, how a
>   condition of re-
>   ceptivity flinches
>   for brightness

>   glare can dazzle
>   no friction like
>   the imbalance
>   of a tree

>   crammed together
>   gleaning the token
>   as though crusts
>   of the radiance
>   could subside
>   its own bark

>   Forest to shuttle a gate of light, select receivers
>   apply vertical rind   wireless bright, deep
>   branch conduction, the cambium's
>   entire battery of reserve

Sheeted, not sheathed, in localities of light-
fall   is there a leeside which only a stubborn
vertical could portend?

11

Light plies saplings by inches, coarsly aiding
the spares   atonement for anything vaster
yet, a day's light

                A stubble of reception shone its diagonal
                prism, glimmers a vertical
                seedling

        every diminished
        rank highlit
        like skulls
        in the sun

        so slender a
        lumen forms
        upright coil
        on the gentlest
        bulb of twig

        a stratum of
        dearth moved to
        glint, arrowing
        among spires

        tree-crown
        in its contented
        wintry steeps

                A crust to the glaze, as it is strewn within
                fittings of tree   the turntable of site
                to light

Not that crowns were bare of light but
they have their vertical
mask

12

Trees in a coat of light, iridescent upward
not of their own making   irregular plateau
of gift at their own marking

                    Shines along the core of outstretched
                    limb   even quicker start than a
                    vertical taper

            pyramidal excess
            equally near each
            parcel of light:
            grant pine

            conspicuous punches
            of light, inside
            the lift of a
            tree-house

            a glimmer of
            fragments
            escaping
            home shade

                    Never sheer horizontals across the field of
                    light   must come to a vertical ramp of
                    occurrence

Entrust light to spin a ground of sky, poly-
focal tree-flame   unconditional local
climb

13

Slow branches traffic an angle, streeting
a further junction lightward

                    Feral spray, brittle-jointed on the flow of
                    light   for all stumpage, bluntly stands
                    bright

          whip tall
          by burrowing
          into light

          instinct radials
          within a novelty
          of branch-cage

          to necessary
          nurture any tree
          will have braided
          its finishing
          touch

                    Expelled by light and become the less or
                    more of their own upshot reserves

Only a crown's transpiration can elate the
sector-ratios of participant light

14

What can be spared of light is what a forest
most belongs to   unfixed spars in tight
orientation

                      Nothing dark settles the reliance other than
                      disparate sky, nocturnal verticals

            tree-skeleton
            shaped for a
            moon more
            pliable than
            its life-rind

            finite cross-
            participation
            toward singulars
            of vertical trust

            hinterlane not
            wrangling with
            summit, how
            trees convert
            daylight to
            sky

                      May light never stretch the grand plains with
                      scarcely a woodlot towards it

Tree-avid horizontals conspire a vertical
crescendo

15

Majority moribund upright core within a vital
exterior vertical allegory   a tree's minority
forefinger prods taller than its hunger

                      Forest not light-flooded, the sun is fractional
                      like a photo-skeletal heartwood thriving its
                      obstruct-garland

            disturbing woodland
            with scarce tap-
            estries of lift

            shrinking to a
            life prolongs
            outreach, each
            bough photo-
            forwards its
            proto-rigidities

            focal stiffness
            (unstripped-
            ness) in stiller
            curls of light

                      Intact forest barely adjacent to buried bags of
                      light, the spectral intake of woody implant

Illustrate the green portion of leavable
light, its post-visibility   assist a pre-forest
vulnerable halo

UNTIL UNDER
A WOOD FORGET
HOW THE HEDGE WARPS

THE SINGULARITY

ITS ATMOSPHERIC WARP

ALREADY PASSED AS HOLY

Lissa Wolsak

Topographic Note

These poems arose out of fascination with a small stretch of shattered but re-vaulting former beech-hedge now itself immersed under the edge of Westridge Wood on the side which skirts Waterley Bottom and adjoining the Tyndale Monument (Gloucestershire) on the other.

1

Along a snagged hull
under full crown flotation

                                The longest outfall   no sagging
                                off a never tepid shave

                untwistable swathe
                ever earlier non-
                deviations from line

                a new (near) wandering
                in full clutch of
                holding to wound

                enwombs this para-
                lytic bulge, captures
                windings, in caption
                to strange drawings
                from bind

                          The copse chokes once, then flows
                          over its prelimits, peripheral permits

Palpable relapse onto demarcation
without the slightest eclipse
of copse

2

Capped as ruptured, rolls out along
crags nurturing its cribbed pace,
a cradle of redressed (unmobbed)
stabbings

        Immediate verticals (ventricals) of hedge-line
        never to focus unless shortened to this
        newly congealed (furnished) enrolment

    how thrown from vertical
    rebuds along sheer
    congested horizontal

    post-hedging
    robbed onto pledge:
    a cramped linear
    enwraps its hinge

    a tree-wake
    swoops once again
    to vertical lesions

        Roots fought for edge (boundary brilliance)
        ahead of what sowing was pending
        in the midst of   how to be cut
        to barrier

Abandoned in ossified glint
of sourceful revision, post-
original incision

3

A space of subtraction (same things) realised a
meta-tract compiled from not severing the
de-rangement

                      Diverse pillage abets local striation,
                      bloating the ration of structure

          in blank sprig
          its outing, clouded
          garnish, *as* blunted
          hunts beyond
          entrapment,
          absconds the why
          of a hedge-forcer

          gnarled notation,
          hurled (unreleased)
          rotation

          fleeting terrace
          floating missing
          verticals, fresher at
          curtalling

          whole twists
          retemper
          the persistence

                    Creases with sudden (unsodden shelter)
                    consents, deeper into the woodedge
                    than trees have a delimit for

Exactly summitless in hedge archaeology,
this wrap-relic could never resemble
a ruined tree

4

The pleat (plant) of distortion is retentive,
a crust of attestive transmission, elongated
into intimacy, enrocks the cradle of a slash

        Long interrupted, counter-blunted, out-
        growing its compaction link   woodland
        becomes pure overhang at this no longer
        dejection of rim

    post-reclusive
    however a less
    than admittance

    that the hedge's
    fore-betrayal
    might wed the
    thread of woods

    transmemberment
    of tree thong

    unsolitary fragment
    tunnelling (circulating)
    inevitable canopy

        A hedge-sector needs newly bestow pristine
        verticals it can never rake amid
        a copse's universal thickening

Less wounded while regraining arbitrary
horizontals, still feeds the granulations finding
vertical cable, fronds the unpleat

5

New filters paring at the desertion/insertion lanes,
swelling (squirreling) inclusion onto
sheer (sheared) intendance

                Already the copse sided with linear-extract,
                boundary-parodied, what exactly drifts into
                confine, a hedge's pre-crush storming at brush

        trees-from-hedge
        spill nothing
        worse, an under-
        vaulting given
        staccato bush
        across the copse's
        full dressage

        drowse on the petal-
        less woodsheen,
        covered light
        grains its favour
        without splitting
        the knots

                Hedge is a refusal prong which up-braids
                an unrecalcitrant disparate overhang

More untakeable that a hedge-relic was left
to the furtive-growth horizons
of its wrecked defensive

6

Because shelter must be borne with, struck down
by   has its oppressions (rammed norms)
of engaging the nurture

                Receivable dislocation whose aftermath
                argues (its) more plentiful contiguities

        whose gaps are
        trenched and seasoned
        by this index
        of delay

        guidance only
        voided (englobed)
        at the same
        temperate
        sprouting bubble,
        pioneer huddle

        open detention-
        valves now
        filter the wood's
        crown estimate

                Copse-shade the greater allows a ruined hedge
                to mine its vein, encapsulate a greeted
                semi-cradle of welcome

Hedge-skirmished parabolas of invention scaled
by entire copse   a vehicle at its register
pleads the drag

7

Not a bound figure but ventures a resendable off hedge-
bounce (bunch) as where cut to obsolete definition
nothing is rescinded other than this travelling
punctuation of recess

                        The errancy retains its over-shaven, slippery
                        currency, simply wanders wounded without
                        squandering

                active para-remnant
                green to the very
                extortion, infolds
                a new comprising
                (compressed)

                flesh of a snare
                open to fresh
                leash, signifying
                copse from
                just such a
                rooted trip-wire

                hedge without
                a bite, except
                where marked
                by its own
                snag teeth

No enribbed contortion without overhang directly
blinking (sinking) light, palely as the counter-
reach entails it

Slender upper norms (beech) retremble the wizened
boundary steps   knew stabbings that repaid
a pure interior network price

8

Greenwood razed to green gear (hedge bone)
gives direct gaze (gauze) from the rim

        Risk is circumference, a boundary-cut (shaded
        out)
        rests in its own figure of definitive docking

    widening of wound
    from sheer transect

    least amplitude
    wouldn't leave
    a pimple
    save for this
    wounding
    until outline

    the glint of a
    cut across
    illocality

        Frankest in deep striation, in being cut down
        to reversed source   even this an overgrowth
        revises but never de-concises

Not rubbed away but ribbed the way of
bristling ghost, as across the whole
gust of woodland

9

The collar of this copse is a snaffled
ribbon, bloated clues to repose, in-
cisions uncontended

                Remains of hedge at wrest, exclamation of its
                dearth in swollen knees

        virtual blight
        of alignment
        offers strict
        over-wooded
        shore

        stopful, a crease
        within the copse's
        free contouring,
        bitter rootal
        re/sign
        of connection

                The stance of the hedge still echoic
                however rashly appointed

Broad to the slights of primal adjustive
twist: semi-withdrawal, a prayer sparser
than its inordinates

10

Stranger compulsions of relief haunt self-
sown adolescent beech, an inverse trench
reserves its own damage reception,
core bombardment

                      Still growing from the verticality wrung
                      out of it, a new imploratory thrown at
                      progressive blockage

          arabesque
          boxed in crust,
          crystalline in
          minute swerve
          under/around
          currents of
          archaic slash

          the after-graft
          of its non-
          disappearance

          post-creature
          patterns of
          resorting to
          hedging

                      Let it disarrange from that, a specific
                      less amid the copse's profusion, intact growth
                      parameter, deep-gouge gutter   greenline
                      batters (matters) in finesse

Only there traduced fixation can set an entire
copse oscillating again   now its swaying crowns
rattle with location

11

Grasp the ratios of attendance according to
some interior grating   even before a breeze
sits in the trees

                      This sub-scab may be super-cherished along a
                      ruse of untapped general growth   generosity
                      attains the level of hedge-snub, universal pivot

          non-invasive
          disfunction
          lifts conflict
          out of the trees

          post-encumbrance
          model of future
          elations, at
          this snagged
          collation of en-
          gulfed first
          fitting

          short on source,
          long on recess,
          reverticalises
          from an offshoot

                    Shaped to a lost (doesn't toss) connection,
                    blunt
                    tiller how the copse runs its course

Reaches into the stark, how easily forked,
how gently stumped   that the hedge's startled
post-contortions are the wood's core attendants

12

Bedding out what has passed on its counter-
cage, direct continuance across
obsolete reclamation

        Speculative at remnant, knots need to
        experiment
        in swollen findings

    excussive non-
    explosive, fugal
    meta-individuation

    chopped hedge
    layers still
    definitively
    unstrangled

    the figment
    unexiled
    never without
    its tools

        Mutating the proportion between boundary
        stock
        and semi-subsequent (vertical) bracing

Meditative bearings but no clearing
other than clipping the copse itself

13

Poly-boundary melding hard shutnesses,
no innocence between root and trunk
but fierce (provisional) interlacking

                Shuttles its own brittle parts, full of
                path travelling brusque in kind to copse

        copse's coat
        withinhaps,
        preliminary
        welter

        enwithholding
        only at a beech's
        full street

        doctored-futile
        body, dredged
        to fore-keel

        vascular en-
        velopped, glides
        contours
        relimbing

                Inelastic cusps until co-hidden at
                scarce a diversion *to* tree-canopy

Active residuals, affinities between stormed
copes, how the whole copse shunts
with diagonal correction

14

Pulled through a cage of too many intentions
the hedge was saddled (couched) with a course

                      Swabbing further branch-clues for no more
                      throbbing, now the hedge casts off its decking

Nothing contrastive will regroup a copse
vector, speculate its interior grouping

            precarious ropes
            make for
            steep repair,
            a hedge at its
            prayer-ruff

            disclosive
            measures
            past their own
            contour

            fettered domain
            warring into
            attaining copse

            impingent
            bundle, the
            copse's reserve
            crater

                    Unsoured rods of distortion, a better-twined
                    or groom-all wrap, same cladding for pressing
                    uprights out of gap

To every several seal other thrivings
are owed, the overtaken at its strongest
filter

EXPRESSING TREES BY DEFAULT

Note

However much there is no way of expressing how trees might express themselves, we can speculate on why the psychic debris left over from the attempt is not recoverable but gets drawn into their own field; and not just through a lack of boundaries but by way of a positive ontological generosity. As such the expressive might be being reassembled across dimly and unevenly shared intervals and overlaps from within a freedom of common underwriting which is constantly being loaned onward; re-commended as a prayerful, and not merely excessive, surplus.

Some Sources

John Milbank, 'The Linguistic Turn as a Theological Turn' in his *The Word Made Strange* (1997)
Johann Gottfried Herder, 'Treatise on the Origin of Language' in his *Philosophical Writings* (2002)
David George Haskell, *The Songs of Trees* (2017)
Peter Wohlleben, *The Hidden Life of Trees* (2016)

1

Pressing on less than sought, a more than provided   expressive retrial drying until gasp, branch-particle speaks its soak-away

A maimed in trees unclaimed of their excision, seals the expression, densities are not immensities   the rejoinder to be pared as heard

                    cherished in-
                    visibly despaired
                    until expression does
                    its lesser appearance,
                    extreme non-clearance

                    expresses no self-
                    imputation, 'here
                    we alleviate' remains
                    raw, stands in the one
                    mention between them

                    charred project (voice)
                    inflames leavings, breath-
                    ings, cool canopy

Deters independent elation, conducts, conditions, sails expression by its one bony thing, stipulates its stem

Nothing-bearing if not expressive repairs, what does implant if compressed to spine   lean savour of pause before life seeks sign

2

A germ of outgrowth or low-harm expression, no other real dimming: forest shade brittle buzz (bud) of tree-throat in default of any broader oncoming

Scarce sowing what to express of it   as if compiled to an awkward recurrence, abbreviant tree interview

> notched if capped
> no first *few* fruits
> until sapped (quoted)
> by expressing them
>
> animate-immobile
> spread (spend) of
> signage, shared kinds
> of tree-flesh
>
> forest clearance not yet
> taming the manifestation:
> empty enough on further
> utterable grounds

We have no other expression apart from what fields it speak   not mute but making a brush of its discernment

What stammers universally   unvagrantly migrant, advancing forest discretion at a leap of faulted root   to be no matter but what the ramification whirls, tongues

3

Expressing-tree, slender quasi-participant, rooted across such co-remainder parsings of as, but in direct sign (ring) of embodied branch

Not displaced in its ask a sign but reducible clearance in expressing a contour   the arcing gap hasn't become a tree's thing in itself

>in full fault of its
>counter-absents,
>recess no larger than
>meagre to woodland
>
>a site which doesn't
>exhaust its own
>fleeing, every escape
>is launched
>
>expressing a nothing-
>less as noonday
>nod in branch
>
>take meaning to be
>a grounded vane in
>woods, predicts the
>chips blown onto
>expression

Pressing on repose but not violating exposure, the contiguity which shows off a perfected hurt, protected screech

Fissured meaning nearer than ever in what the trees seek out   full spread pronunciation

4

Express a tree suddenly pleat its own saturation   delicate adjunct ramification through the scarcings of rooted enough

No folding back into the flux of treeing without this stance   newly unredundant tree-vocals, soughing verticals

> questing in leaf-mode
> for stranger, un-
> stronger phrases
>
> split the green gut
> into something within
> flame, but in plain
> recital
>
> probes the parse of it-
> self, incomplete pause
> over the scarcely of
> an unwithdrawn

Acknowledge a tree and exfoliate its name   what it doesn't say but reaches (branches) any account of   perception remains under the bark, as expression is undetaining, not even reframing

A spectral name under eaves in leaf, let it alone with the forest conspectus: a formal virginity of world which trees will be the least to embrace, rather with murmur than for violation

5

What tree else is a sign's whole matter of construction?   true tree distortion its tentative (radial) proportion

A holly-bush overgrows around its sensuous strict setting   no weaving expressive weakness without mouthing trials of entanglement

        treasure abstraction
        from primal stem,
        first chance choices
        of a stammering
        (uneliding) fork

        these wants will have
        ground, if only for a
        single round: a voice
        wrinkles the trees

        tree-naming
        for its enshrouded
        alternative

A tree column's consent or reprisal representation   let it contain definition, offsides attentive to semantic splay

Root-steps onto a slippage of world, stubborn arrest in default of assigned retention   this has always spoken out its ravageful connection

6

Spanning how trees express their former protocols too long in default: hold-down time is encrustment fully pronounced

By default bespeak woods to some semi-origin, however radial in unrecorded release

        naming each feature
        its own ballast,
        default root off
        precurves of branch
        as conversant device

        no atrocity of
        onset, mainly
        the default
        itself

        default value
        not a failure of
        handling but residue
        futures sounding
        integral recession

        why a tree on
        sightless course
        is to press (pimple)
        the intimation

Express it a tree in default of any other resemblance   the analogy is gift-complete

A no-fault ratio of forest to hitherto unseverable clotting of remand, the trees' retreatant console

7

Indurate bespoke branch hybridity so generic in expression, until what it confers

Compound gear won't unsimplify this relapse into trees   here impounded by how receptors sift until a gift of having said the unseeking

>because forest won't
>file a grammatical
>void, its intensive
>prefix forward-
>ing to pastoral
>
>stunned senses
>at a stand of trees,
>this too expresses
>woodland reproach
>
>a naturality-stem even
>when least delicate,
>sufficient web of no
>further bare expression

No wood could hint by default at hidden allies, its horizon out-recedes even such slumped absences of report

Narrowly a circle arborial so to speak branch, always newer, lesser, than global tree

8

A forest's shortcomings speak incompressible gap (lilt), the outflow steeper than ground but towards expressly a transplant

No origin envelops so fully, does express scarcity to an endless colloquy of tree   plenum of the partial, prayerful even more than least from

>   nature gave no force
>   to a vain tree, in-
>   flective intuition
>   off a noise of forest,
>   the brows' terminals
>   hearing the addition
>
>   irregular quavering
>   texture for what
>   insisted, ramifies
>   the exclamation
>
>   meaning their
>   hinterland de-
>   tections: express
>   tree in cross-
>   co-section

Forest self-signage doesn't have enough of a plea to become poor, dimly instils the gift of exposition

A mess of glades/events accumulate a new verbal tree   pre-conjugates reach changed in every reached thing, a thornless wood

9

Weaken the sense to express the poverty of its kind, it still narrates ramific racking and soaring

Expression in the rudiments of tree, not of it   which a forest could have named/disowned as little as it needs to

        boughs without con-
        sent, no such pre-
        vention: presencing
        complicit ramific
        inventives, local
        turmoil of convention

        the run on forest
        seeks another ob-
        ject of declamation,
        traces expressly
        plain or yet to

        and hence for all
        tones of the world, ex-
        pressive twig to
        traverse a single
        conversant particle

Natural ploy offering strong sense to the weaknesses of a whole communicating series   how a tree is sprig-like commonly about its hyper-source

One sole emplaced cry for the continuing species   trees lacking any relay save their cloaks of expression   assumes a language of bestowal within its branch-degrees

10

Aridly a tree's store of creation not so restrained in enduring its tumours of expression   post-random office against an effacing world, offends instant predator affix

Making interior what can't evenly recess into themselves   expression is woodland's contrary spread, signed contraction

        assuming they form
        nothing more than
        tree-borrowings, con-
        tingent small bringings
        among elementary
        silent signs

        any nodule artefact
        selected in tree,
        the tabbed panel
        notched expressively

        how a tree congeals
        taking emplacement
        as its there-expression

        more liquidly
        woodland-aware,
        a flush off forest
        plying its ambushed
        running signs

Expressly betrays a code-ripple sounding off tree-surfaces   for its own hollowness sake not just dissembling

This is the element of common summons   default-driven to exacerbate a depth of prepending tree

11

In sessions of its restart, sudden expedition of design, making a murmur out of its underseries   captioned (full leaf) across fractals of lessened inexpression

Forest cross-validation, confers from the main set as of many trees, expressive texture by few valves, furnished field

> communicant estimator
> in default of random
> forest, explicit terrace
>
> tree-needful signal
> to its own sails, leafage
> in the trial of recognition
>
> a scab index
> left by a common
> spine of message

A smattering of collective onus across punctured syntax   with expression this rare, it slips into attachment

Configured spray unnative upon its own expression, senses what microbranches towards translating amendments to horizon

12

Even a forest's thoughts have intake for spare (spannable) accomplishments, accounts them trans-recessive

Share the distortion of trees with their own self-tampering accent, ellipses and gift

>here is silence
>throwing a light spasm
>beyond itself
>
>leaves it to a
>forest-choric
>in voiced assault
>
>aligned (secreted)
>to spoken on a
>wordless ratio

Quote a tree and trepidate its life-source, harmless if only sentenced to the brinks in branching

A read datum disturbed from minimal depth   breathes its attentiveness, tree surviving arrivals of tree

13

Dash of signalling (molecular) towards acoustic reckoning, panic signifiers until sparer (spired) at tree-crown

Lopping the wood from a tree is forest topping its credences   canopy apex becomes a horizontal vocabulary

>no strain of voice
>comes from it,
>simply a slight
>compatible gain
>
>expended documentary
>forest with nothing
>to sing, the arboreal record
>already made
>
>in perpetual
>thin film
>explicates horizon

A symbolics of tree-squandered semiotics, at this last filter sent scarce, half-perish the expression

Thins out language by root as nature subjects its resource-stomata to expressive reduction   the level at which gift-precedence can be deciphered a tree at a time

14

Tree: offers contrivance a re-embowering (drastic) horizon it was this rectification that scanted interpretation, prods adequate centre-zero, additive praying hollow

If a wood ever did inflect its timbres, such a telling rage would see its substance transmuted

>or signals galvanize
>languid concurrence,
>diffuse-direct uni-
>versal plant connection
>
>a forest speaks to
>its modernity, rudi-
>mentary conversation
>between plant and
>unpickable knot
>
>tree-calm con-
>vulsive expression,
>optimum slows (un-
>slewed) of meaning

Small local talk part of the forest's larger hunger of thought, infused switches, swathes seeking behaviour

The trees won't hiss their way to expression but wherever there is long, corrosive, soft bite

15

Tilt their heads away from the crying atom, rely on a filtered wash of expression   sprinkles its own complaint on the initiation

Meaning the narrow-turn interlude, interstitial harmonics amid their amplificatory churning of void   a tree will respeak this for immediate repose, slender pauses of the spirit within its micro-vouch connection, not yet pushing life ahead of life

> in forests of an
> only life common
> to commentary
>
> thin-film net-
> worked irreversibles,
> communication failure
> not in itself un-
> knotted, unsaid
>
> intent weak enough
> for a mild haze
> of preference
> over the forest

Narrow (newer) signatures are styles of drought, scarce co-efficients of brittle sensation in compression

Fullness on the edge of material unmet demand, ribbed extras of petition

16

At the tree-hoot stabilize the aggregate, let its unconditionals sparkle a time-gap, penultimate dip as horizon murmurs a sufficiency of scale scarcity expresses its decelerant allowables, follows the award

Nonetheless a halo of encouraged signal, chimera against blank concentrations   carries hard messages up to its own stressors, a buffer-zone gets to be pre-informed

        leaves simultaneous
        adepts at counter-
        assault, awake to
        inner shocks vocally
        seeking the valve

        network speaks mutuals
        beyond their beds, a
        catalyst in *not*
        offloading local
        control even as
        pervious root beckons
        from crevice to loop

        how the wood
        is met in its
        expression, strands
        of meta-congregation

Trees within the swamp of every other congregation's news   predatory undertow waits for its partial summation

Allies of distressed woodland   not now its expressive but its receptive disuse of external moan

17

Any express-arboreal in not over-presenting (hyper-venting) but undergoes its own lessened (seasoned) re-approach

Curtails (curves) in retention a relief of opposite ground, until only the expression of it caverns openly, deeper rebound than the gate itself

       diffuses its brace
       back across the ex-
       pulsive swirl of
       fence: clamped tree
       is perceptive stance,
       excerptive ramp

       leanness is full
       participation declaring
       the scarcity of
       association

       such vouching despite
       mute assembly
       is tree-work, what
       the default does stammer
       but won't shirk

       every stem-word
       has a sign-familiar
       listening to leaf

Woodland relics came from over the horizon, same sown origins sing reblown stringing   to interpret the sample drone of a tree in leaf

A stiffness of tree-tongue shapes beneath local intervals   a correlation of tone with local bodings of root

Meaning that a scarcity obstinates (places) its clearing   stringent blockade tokenly expressed (refreshed) in trees spoken

18

What the cheek learns against a wood by touch   unavoidability, then expressive lag of reception

Wires a tree without crackling its abatements   tree-to-human along the amply-shed pathway into thinking the sonics

        tree-worded, proves
        in literal messages
        vital attenuation,
        slip of bough

        a voice untangled by
        its echoes, at ultra-
        slow freshly livable,
        newly assigns its near-
        est symbolic hindrance

        will flock to trees
        despite their
        trapped attachments

Ripe at the forest's own narrative, shapes a beyond-human commonality, or a vertical and humanly beyond   shares across a slope of gift

Prefoliar in tapping junctions of signlessness   onto a heard silence of meta-extent, sudden quota of expressive event

www.ingramcontent.com/pod-product-compliance
Lightning Source LLC
Chambersburg PA
CBHW021327190426
43193CB00039B/414